GOOD FOR YOU!

A WELLNESS PLANNER FOR HEALTHY & HAPPY LIVING

JON MOORE

CASTLE POINT BOOKS

NEW YORK

THIS PLANNER BELONGS TO:

....

We turn
NOT OLDER
WITH YEARS
but NEWER
every day.

—Emily Dickinson

Every day is full of new opportunities to prioritize your wellness. From your morning thoughts that set the tone for the day to the foods and activities that fill the hours after, you have the power to create the healthy, happy, balanced lifestyle you want. Don't get stuck in the tendency to wait for the right time—your time is now, and the support is in your hands!

Good for You! is your daily reminder to make the best choices for your physical, mental, and emotional well-being—aiming for sustainable over perfect to see a real difference in your energy, wellness, and mindset. Find motivation as you develop daily habits for health and happiness, including:

POSITIVE THOUGHTS: **Boost your wellness efforts and self-love with the right mindset.**

ACTIVE DAY: **Celebrate both structured exercise and simple movement throughout the day.**

CLEAR MIND: **Find space to drop whatever is weighing you down.**

ENERGIZING CHOICES: **Track your water, sleep, fresh-air time, and more—your self-care adds up!**

INTENTIONAL EATING: **Make a plan to fuel your satisfaction and nutrition goals.**

REFLECTION: **Record wellness wins and recognize areas with room for improvement.**

With easy-to-use daily planner pages and a colorful design, *Good for You!* makes it simple and fun to take charge of your wellness and stay committed to a healthier lifestyle.

POSITIVE THOUGHTS

Start your day with an affirmation or intention that prepares you to soar.

ACTIVE DAY

Promise to give your body the gift of movement (casual or structured) and note how you feel when you follow through.

CLEAR MIND

Drop all those distracting to-dos on paper so your head isn't swimming with mental lists.

ENERGIZING CHOICES

TIME IN NATURE

Seek opportunities for fresh air and vitamin D in your every day.

SOCIAL CONNECTIONS

Make time to reach out—even a text—and track how it makes you feel.

BRAIN BOOSTS

Celebrate time spent in brain games, books, and more.

SELF CHECK-INS

Choose a few times throughout the day to stop, breathe, and check in with your feelings.

JOY & GRATITUDE

Schedule a time-out for gratitude or jot down what moves you throughout the day.

RESTFUL SLEEP

Track whatever is important to you—maybe hours in bed, your qualitative assessment, or sticking to a before-bed routine.

INTENTIONAL EATING

Some categories may work better to plan ahead and others may lend to tracking throughout the day. Use these hints to get started, but remember that your planning and tracking need to work for one person: *you*!

BREAKFAST

Plan your fuel and make any notes or adjustments throughout the day.

LUNCH

DINNER

SNACKS

WELL-WATERED

GOOD FOR YOU!

At the end of the day, recognize even little steps you take toward feeling healthier and happier.

KEEP TRYING

Look for areas of improvement or opportunity.

WAKE UP THAT WATER!
ADD SLICES OF LEMON, LIME, ORANGE,
OR CUCUMBER, OR TRY SPRIGS OF MINT
OR LEMON BALM.

POSITIVE THOUGHTS

ACTIVE DAY

CLEAR MIND

ENERGIZING CHOICES

TIME IN NATURE

....
....
....

SOCIAL CONNECTIONS

....
....
....

BRAIN BOOSTS

....
....

SELF CHECK-INS

....
....
....

JOY & GRATITUDE

....
....
....

RESTFUL SLEEP

....
....
....

INTENTIONAL EATING

BREAKFAST

....
....
....

LUNCH

....
....
....

DINNER

....
....
....

SNACKS

....
....
....

WELL-WATERED

○ ○ ○ ○ ○ ○ ○ ○ ○ ○ ○ ○

GOOD FOR YOU!

....
....
....
....

KEEP TRYING

....
....
....
....

EVERY SMALL POSITIVE CHANGE WE
MAKE IN OURSELVES REPAYS US IN
CONFIDENCE IN THE FUTURE.

–ALICE WALKER

POSITIVE THOUGHTS

ACTIVE DAY

CLEAR MIND

ENERGIZING CHOICES

TIME IN NATURE

....

....

....

SOCIAL CONNECTIONS

....

....

....

BRAIN BOOSTS

....

....

....

SELF CHECK-INS

....

....

....

JOY & GRATITUDE

....

....

....

RESTFUL SLEEP

....

....

....

INTENTIONAL EATING

BREAKFAST

....
....
....

LUNCH

....
....
....

DINNER

....
....
....

SNACKS

....
....
....

WELL-WATERED

GOOD FOR YOU!

....
....
....
....

KEEP TRYING

....
....
....
....

SET A DATE.
BEEN PROMISING TO GET TOGETHER "SOON" WITH
SOMEONE SPECIAL IN YOUR LIFE? AGREE ON A DATE
AND GET IT ON YOUR CALENDARS TODAY.

POSITIVE THOUGHTS

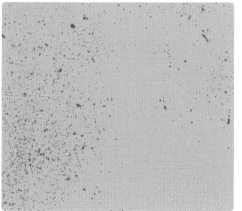

ACTIVE DAY

CLEAR MIND

ENERGIZING CHOICES

TIME IN NATURE

....

....

....

SOCIAL CONNECTIONS

....

....

....

BRAIN BOOSTS

....

....

....

SELF CHECK-INS

....

....

....

JOY & GRATITUDE

....

....

....

RESTFUL SLEEP

....

....

....

INTENTIONAL EATING

BREAKFAST

....

....

....

LUNCH

....

....

....

DINNER

....

....

....

SNACKS

....

....

....

WELL-WATERED

○ ○ ○ ○ ○ ○ ○ ○ ○ ○ ○ ○

GOOD FOR YOU!

....

....

....

....

KEEP TRYING

....

....

....

....

THERE CAN BE NO HAPPINESS IF THE THINGS
WE BELIEVE IN ARE DIFFERENT FROM
THE THINGS WE DO.

—FREYA STARK

DATE .... M T W TH F SAT SUN

POSITIVE THOUGHTS

ACTIVE DAY

CLEAR MIND

ENERGIZING CHOICES

TIME IN NATURE

....

....

....

SOCIAL CONNECTIONS

....

....

....

BRAIN BOOSTS

....

....

....

SELF CHECK-INS

....

....

....

JOY & GRATITUDE

....

....

....

RESTFUL SLEEP

....

....

....

INTENTIONAL EATING

BREAKFAST

....

....

....

DINNER

....

....

....

LUNCH

....

....

....

SNACKS

....

....

....

WELL-WATERED

○ ○ ○ ○ ○ ○ ○ ○ ○ ○ ○ ○

GOOD FOR YOU!

....

....

....

....

....

KEEP TRYING

....

....

....

....

....

CATCH YOUR BREATH.
AVOID BUYING INTO BUSYNESS AS A BADGE OF
HONOR. GIVE YOURSELF POCKETS OF TIME
EACH DAY TO SIMPLY BREATHE OR WATCH THE
CLOUDS GO BY.

DATE .... M T W TH F SAT SUN

POSITIVE THOUGHTS

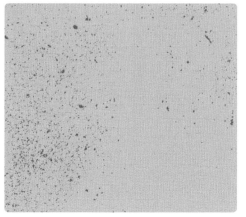

ENERGIZING CHOICES

TIME IN NATURE

....
....
....

SOCIAL CONNECTIONS

....
....
....

ACTIVE DAY

BRAIN BOOSTS

....
....
....

SELF CHECK-INS

....
....
....

CLEAR MIND

JOY & GRATITUDE

....
....
....

RESTFUL SLEEP

....
....
....

INTENTIONAL EATING

BREAKFAST

....

....

....

LUNCH

....

....

....

DINNER

....

....

....

SNACKS

....

....

....

WELL-WATERED

○ ○ ○ ○ ○ ○ ○ ○ ○ ○ ○ ○

GOOD FOR YOU!

....

....

....

....

KEEP TRYING

....

....

....

....

WE CAN CLIMB MOUNTAINS
WITH SELF-LOVE.

−SAMIRA WILEY

DATE .... M T W TH F SAT SUN

POSITIVE THOUGHTS

ACTIVE DAY

CLEAR MIND

ENERGIZING CHOICES

TIME IN NATURE

....

....

....

SOCIAL CONNECTIONS

....

....

....

BRAIN BOOSTS

....

....

....

SELF CHECK-INS

....

....

....

JOY & GRATITUDE

....

....

....

RESTFUL SLEEP

....

....

....

INTENTIONAL EATING

BREAKFAST

....
....
....

LUNCH

....
....
....

DINNER

....
....
....

SNACKS

....
....
....

WELL-WATERED

○ ○ ○ ○ ○ ○ ○ ○ ○ ○ ○ ○

GOOD FOR YOU!

....
....
....
....

KEEP TRYING

....
....
....
....

RESIST FOOD REWARDS.
INSTEAD OF CONNECTING WHAT YOU EAT
TO WHAT YOU ACCOMPLISH, BASE YOUR FOOD
DECISIONS ON WHAT MAKES YOU FEEL
STRONG AND SATISFIED.

DATE .... M T W TH F SAT SUN

POSITIVE THOUGHTS

ACTIVE DAY

CLEAR MIND

ENERGIZING CHOICES

TIME IN NATURE

....

....

....

SOCIAL CONNECTIONS

....

....

BRAIN BOOSTS

....

....

SELF CHECK-INS

....

....

JOY & GRATITUDE

....

....

RESTFUL SLEEP

....

....

INTENTIONAL EATING

BREAKFAST

....

....

....

LUNCH

....

....

....

DINNER

....

....

....

SNACKS

....

....

....

WELL-WATERED

GOOD FOR YOU!

....

....

....

....

KEEP TRYING

....

....

....

....

I CAN AND I WILL.
WATCH ME.

-CARRIE GREEN

DATE .... M T W TH F SAT SUN

POSITIVE THOUGHTS

ENERGIZING CHOICES

TIME IN NATURE

....

....

....

SOCIAL CONNECTIONS

....

....

....

ACTIVE DAY

BRAIN BOOSTS

....

....

....

SELF CHECK-INS

....

....

....

CLEAR MIND

JOY & GRATITUDE

....

....

....

RESTFUL SLEEP

....

....

....

INTENTIONAL EATING

BREAKFAST

....

....

....

DINNER

....

....

....

LUNCH

....

....

....

SNACKS

....

....

....

WELL-WATERED

GOOD FOR YOU!

....

....

....

....

....

KEEP TRYING

....

....

....

....

....

HANG OUT WITH POSITIVE PEOPLE.
IT'S EASIER TO STICK WITH GOOD-FOR-YOU CHOICES
WHEN YOU'RE SPENDING TIME WITH ENCOURAGING
FRIENDS WHO ARE PRIORITIZING WELLNESS, TOO.

POSITIVE THOUGHTS

ACTIVE DAY

CLEAR MIND

ENERGIZING CHOICES

TIME IN NATURE

....

....

....

SOCIAL CONNECTIONS

....

....

....

BRAIN BOOSTS

....

....

....

SELF CHECK-INS

....

....

....

JOY & GRATITUDE

....

....

....

RESTFUL SLEEP

....

....

....

INTENTIONAL EATING

BREAKFAST

LUNCH

....

....

....

....

....

....

DINNER

SNACKS

....

....

....

....

....

....

WELL-WATERED

GOOD FOR YOU!

KEEP TRYING

....

....

....

....

....

....

....

....

....

....

CONTINUOUS IMPROVEMENT IS BETTER
THAN DELAYED PERFECTION.

-MARK TWAIN

POSITIVE THOUGHTS

ACTIVE DAY

CLEAR MIND

ENERGIZING CHOICES

TIME IN NATURE

....

....

....

SOCIAL CONNECTIONS

....

....

....

BRAIN BOOSTS

....

....

....

SELF CHECK-INS

....

....

....

JOY & GRATITUDE

....

....

....

RESTFUL SLEEP

....

....

....

INTENTIONAL EATING

BREAKFAST

....

....

....

LUNCH

....

....

....

DINNER

....

....

....

SNACKS

....

....

....

WELL-WATERED

○ ○ ○ ○ ○ ○ ○ ○ ○ ○ ○ ○

GOOD FOR YOU!

....

....

....

....

KEEP TRYING

....

....

....

....

CONNECT WITH CALM.
WHEN YOU FEEL ANXIETY RAMPING UP, STOP AND
NOTICE IN THAT MOMENT WHAT YOU CAN FEEL, HEAR,
SEE, SMELL, AND TASTE.

DATE .... M T W TH F SAT SUN

POSITIVE THOUGHTS

ACTIVE DAY

CLEAR MIND

ENERGIZING CHOICES

TIME IN NATURE

....

....

....

SOCIAL CONNECTIONS

....

....

....

BRAIN BOOSTS

....

....

SELF CHECK-INS

....

....

....

JOY & GRATITUDE

....

....

....

RESTFUL SLEEP

....

....

....

INTENTIONAL EATING

BREAKFAST

....

....

....

LUNCH

....

....

....

DINNER

....

....

....

SNACKS

....

....

....

WELL-WATERED

○ ○ ○ ○ ○ ○ ○ ○ ○ ○ ○ ○

GOOD FOR YOU!

....

....

....

....

KEEP TRYING

....

....

....

....

IF YOU TRULY POUR YOUR HEART INTO
WHAT YOU BELIEVE IN, EVEN IF IT MAKES
YOU VULNERABLE, AMAZING THINGS CAN
AND WILL HAPPEN.

–EMMA WATSON

DATE .... M T W TH F SAT SUN

POSITIVE THOUGHTS

ACTIVE DAY

CLEAR MIND

ENERGIZING CHOICES

TIME IN NATURE

....
....
....

SOCIAL CONNECTIONS

....
....
....

BRAIN BOOSTS

....
....
....

SELF CHECK-INS

....
....
....

JOY & GRATITUDE

....
....

RESTFUL SLEEP

....
....

INTENTIONAL EATING

BREAKFAST

....

....

....

LUNCH

....

....

....

DINNER

....

....

....

SNACKS

....

....

....

WELL-WATERED

○ ○ ○ ○ ○ ○ ○ ○ ○ ○ ○ ○

GOOD FOR YOU!

....

....

....

....

KEEP TRYING

....

....

....

....

MOTIVATE YOURSELF WITH VISUAL CUES.
TRYING TO GET MORE MOVEMENT?
KEEP YOUR SNEAKERS IN VIEW. MORE WATER?
TREAT YOURSELF TO A GORGEOUS NEW
WATER BOTTLE.

POSITIVE THOUGHTS

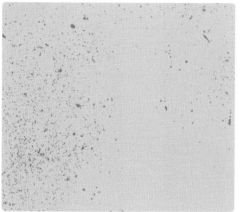

ENERGIZING CHOICES

TIME IN NATURE

....

....

....

SOCIAL CONNECTIONS

....

....

....

ACTIVE DAY

BRAIN BOOSTS

....

....

....

SELF CHECK-INS

....

....

....

CLEAR MIND

JOY & GRATITUDE

....

....

....

RESTFUL SLEEP

....

....

....

INTENTIONAL EATING

BREAKFAST

....

....

....

LUNCH

....

....

....

DINNER

....

....

....

SNACKS

....

....

....

WELL-WATERED

○ ○ ○ ○ ○ ○ ○ ○ ○ ○ ○ ○

GOOD FOR YOU!

....

....

....

....

....

KEEP TRYING

....

....

....

....

....

KEEP GOOD COMPANY, READ GOOD BOOKS,
LOVE GOOD THINGS, AND CULTIVATE SOUL AND
BODY AS FAITHFULLY AS YOU CAN.

—LOUISA MAY ALCOTT

DATE .... M T W TH F SAT SUN

POSITIVE THOUGHTS

ACTIVE DAY

CLEAR MIND

ENERGIZING CHOICES

TIME IN NATURE
....
....
....

SOCIAL CONNECTIONS
....
....
....

BRAIN BOOSTS
....
....
....

SELF CHECK-INS
....
....
....

JOY & GRATITUDE
....
....
....

RESTFUL SLEEP
....
....
....

INTENTIONAL EATING

BREAKFAST

....

....

....

LUNCH

....

....

....

DINNER

....

....

....

SNACKS

....

....

....

WELL-WATERED

○ ○ ○ ○ ○ ○ ○ ○ ○ ○ ○ ○

GOOD FOR YOU!

....

....

....

....

KEEP TRYING

....

....

....

....

GO SLOW.
DO SOMETHING MORE SLOWLY TODAY—IMMERSE
YOURSELF IN COOKING A MEAL FROM SCRATCH OR
MAKING YOUR OWN COFFEE OR JUST WALKING
AT A LEISURELY PACE, TAKING IN THE WORLD
AROUND YOU.

DATE .... M T W TH F SAT SUN

POSITIVE THOUGHTS

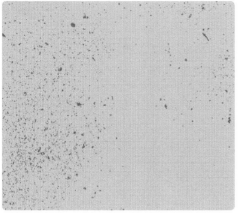

ACTIVE DAY

CLEAR MIND

ENERGIZING CHOICES

TIME IN NATURE

....

....

....

SOCIAL CONNECTIONS

....

....

....

BRAIN BOOSTS

....

....

....

SELF CHECK-INS

....

....

....

JOY & GRATITUDE

....

....

....

RESTFUL SLEEP

....

....

....

INTENTIONAL EATING

BREAKFAST	LUNCH
....	....
....	....
....	....

DINNER	SNACKS
....	....
....	....
....	....

WELL-WATERED

○ ○ ○ ○ ○ ○ ○ ○ ○ ○ ○ ○

GOOD FOR YOU!	KEEP TRYING
....	....
....	....
....	....
....	....

A GOOD LAUGH AND A LONG SLEEP ARE
THE BEST CURES IN THE DOCTOR'S BOOK.

–IRISH PROVERB

DATE .... M T W TH F SAT SUN

POSITIVE THOUGHTS

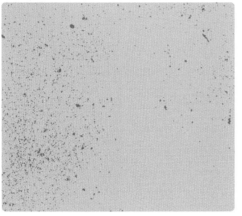

ACTIVE DAY

CLEAR MIND

ENERGIZING CHOICES

TIME IN NATURE

....

....

....

SOCIAL CONNECTIONS

....

....

....

BRAIN BOOSTS

....

....

....

SELF CHECK-INS

....

....

....

JOY & GRATITUDE

....

....

....

RESTFUL SLEEP

....

....

....

INTENTIONAL EATING

BREAKFAST

....

....

....

DINNER

....

....

....

LUNCH

....

....

....

SNACKS

....

....

....

WELL-WATERED

〇 〇 〇 〇 〇 〇 〇 〇 〇 〇 〇 〇

GOOD FOR YOU!

....

....

....

....

KEEP TRYING

....

....

....

....

START A VISION BOARD.
NO MATTER YOUR CURRENT FRONT-AND-CENTER GOAL,
POST WORDS AND IMAGES THAT MOTIVATE YOU TO
KEEP MOVING TOWARD THE PRIZE.

POSITIVE THOUGHTS

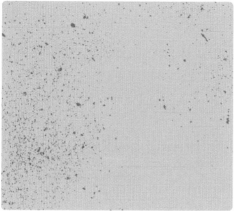

ACTIVE DAY

CLEAR MIND

ENERGIZING CHOICES

TIME IN NATURE

....

....

....

SOCIAL CONNECTIONS

....

....

....

BRAIN BOOSTS

....

....

....

SELF CHECK-INS

....

....

....

JOY & GRATITUDE

....

....

....

RESTFUL SLEEP

....

....

....

INTENTIONAL EATING

BREAKFAST

....

....

....

LUNCH

....

....

....

DINNER

....

....

....

SNACKS

....

....

....

WELL-WATERED

○ ○ ○ ○ ○ ○ ○ ○ ○ ○ ○ ○

GOOD FOR YOU!

....

....

....

....

KEEP TRYING

....

....

....

....

RESPECT YOUR BODY. EAT WELL.
DANCE FOREVER.

–ELIZA GAYNOR MINDEN

DATE .... M T W TH F SAT SUN

POSITIVE THOUGHTS

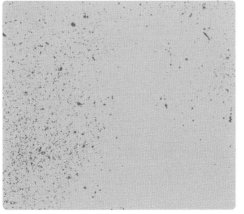

ACTIVE DAY

CLEAR MIND

ENERGIZING CHOICES

TIME IN NATURE

....
....
....

SOCIAL CONNECTIONS

....
....
....

BRAIN BOOSTS

....
....
....

SELF CHECK-INS

....
....
....

JOY & GRATITUDE

....
....
....

RESTFUL SLEEP

....
....
....

INTENTIONAL EATING

BREAKFAST

....

....

....

LUNCH

....

....

....

DINNER

....

....

....

SNACKS

....

....

....

WELL-WATERED

🥛 🥛 🥛 🥛 🥛 🥛 🥛 🥛 🥛 🥛 🥛 🥛

○ ○ ○ ○ ○ ○ ○ ○ ○ ○ ○ ○

GOOD FOR YOU!

....

....

....

....

KEEP TRYING

....

....

....

....

PICK UP AN INSPIRING BOOK.
POETRY, YOGA, AFFIRMATIONS, PLANT-BASED
COOKING . . . THE TOPIC DOESN'T MATTER AS
LONG AS IT MOVES YOU.

POSITIVE THOUGHTS

ACTIVE DAY

CLEAR MIND

ENERGIZING CHOICES

TIME IN NATURE

....
....
....

SOCIAL CONNECTIONS

....
....
....

BRAIN BOOSTS

....
....
....

SELF CHECK-INS

....
....
....

JOY & GRATITUDE

....
....
....

RESTFUL SLEEP

....
....
....

INTENTIONAL EATING

BREAKFAST
....
....
....

LUNCH
....
....
....

DINNER
....
....
....

SNACKS
....
....
....

WELL-WATERED

○ ○ ○ ○ ○ ○ ○ ○ ○ ○ ○ ○

GOOD FOR YOU!
....
....
....
....

KEEP TRYING
....
....
....
....

WHAT I DREAM OF IS AN
ART OF BALANCE.
—HENRI MATISSE

DATE .... M T W TH F SAT SUN

POSITIVE THOUGHTS

ACTIVE DAY

CLEAR MIND

ENERGIZING CHOICES

TIME IN NATURE
....
....
....

SOCIAL CONNECTIONS
....
....
....

BRAIN BOOSTS
....
....
....

SELF CHECK-INS
....
....
....

JOY & GRATITUDE
....
....
....

RESTFUL SLEEP
....
....
....

INTENTIONAL EATING

BREAKFAST

....

....

....

LUNCH

....

....

....

DINNER

....

....

....

SNACKS

....

....

....

WELL-WATERED

◯ ◯ ◯ ◯ ◯ ◯ ◯ ◯ ◯ ◯ ◯ ◯

GOOD FOR YOU!

....

....

....

....

KEEP TRYING

....

....

....

....

BARE YOUR FEET.
LET THEM CONNECT WITH WHATEVER IS BENEATH
THEM—SHAGGY CARPET, SOFT GRASS, OR WARM
SAND. FOCUS ON FEELING GROUNDED AND
DROPPING THE STRESSES OF THE DAY.

DATE .... M T W TH F SAT SUN

POSITIVE THOUGHTS

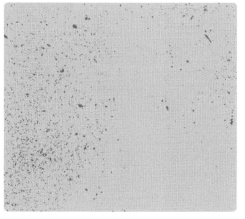

ENERGIZING CHOICES

TIME IN NATURE

....
....
....

SOCIAL CONNECTIONS

....
....
....

ACTIVE DAY

BRAIN BOOSTS

....
....
....

SELF CHECK-INS

....
....
....

CLEAR MIND

JOY & GRATITUDE

....
....
....

RESTFUL SLEEP

....
....
....

INTENTIONAL EATING

BREAKFAST

LUNCH

DINNER

SNACKS

WELL-WATERED

GOOD FOR YOU!

KEEP TRYING

WHEN YOU RECOVER OR DISCOVER SOMETHING
THAT NOURISHES YOUR SOUL AND BRINGS JOY,
CARE ENOUGH ABOUT YOURSELF TO MAKE
ROOM FOR IT IN YOUR LIFE.

–JEAN SHINODA BOLEN

POSITIVE THOUGHTS

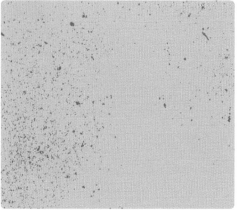

ACTIVE DAY

CLEAR MIND

ENERGIZING CHOICES

TIME IN NATURE

....

....

....

SOCIAL CONNECTIONS

....

....

....

BRAIN BOOSTS

....

....

....

SELF CHECK-INS

....

....

....

JOY & GRATITUDE

....

....

....

RESTFUL SLEEP

....

....

....

INTENTIONAL EATING

BREAKFAST

....

....

....

LUNCH

....

....

....

DINNER

....

....

....

SNACKS

....

....

....

WELL-WATERED

○ ○ ○ ○ ○ ○ ○ ○ ○ ○ ○ ○

GOOD FOR YOU!

....

....

....

....

....

KEEP TRYING

....

....

....

....

....

SHOW UP FOR YOUR GOALS.
TAKE ONE SMALL STEP TOWARD A BIG GOAL—SIGN UP
FOR A FITNESS OR COOKING CLASS, OPEN A SPECIAL
SAVINGS ACCOUNT, OR UPDATE YOUR RÉSUMÉ.

DATE .... M T W TH F SAT SUN

POSITIVE THOUGHTS

ACTIVE DAY

CLEAR MIND

ENERGIZING CHOICES

TIME IN NATURE

....
....
....

SOCIAL CONNECTIONS

....
....
....

BRAIN BOOSTS

....
....
....

SELF CHECK-INS

....
....
....

JOY & GRATITUDE

....
....
....

RESTFUL SLEEP

....
....
....

INTENTIONAL EATING

BREAKFAST

....

....

....

LUNCH

....

....

....

DINNER

....

....

....

SNACKS

....

....

....

WELL-WATERED

GOOD FOR YOU!

....

....

....

....

KEEP TRYING

....

....

....

....

YOU ARE ALLOWED TO BE BOTH
A MASTERPIECE AND A WORK IN
PROGRESS, SIMULTANEOUSLY.

–SOPHIA BUSH

POSITIVE THOUGHTS

ENERGIZING CHOICES

TIME IN NATURE

....

....

....

SOCIAL CONNECTIONS

....

....

....

ACTIVE DAY

BRAIN BOOSTS

....

....

....

SELF CHECK-INS

....

....

....

CLEAR MIND

JOY & GRATITUDE

....

....

....

RESTFUL SLEEP

....

....

....

INTENTIONAL EATING

BREAKFAST

....

....

....

LUNCH

....

....

....

DINNER

....

....

....

SNACKS

....

....

....

WELL-WATERED

○ ○ ○ ○ ○ ○ ○ ○ ○ ○ ○ ○

GOOD FOR YOU!

....

....

....

....

....

KEEP TRYING

....

....

....

....

....

SAY YES.

IF AN OPPORTUNITY COMES ALONG THAT FEELS
RIGHT FOR YOU, ENTHUSIASTICALLY SAY YES.
FIGHT THE URGE TO OVERTHINK EVERY DETAIL
OF WHAT MAY OR MAY NOT HAPPEN.

POSITIVE THOUGHTS

ACTIVE DAY

CLEAR MIND

ENERGIZING CHOICES

TIME IN NATURE

....

....

....

SOCIAL CONNECTIONS

....

....

....

BRAIN BOOSTS

....

....

....

SELF CHECK-INS

....

....

....

JOY & GRATITUDE

....

....

....

RESTFUL SLEEP

....

....

....

INTENTIONAL EATING

BREAKFAST

....

....

....

LUNCH

....

....

....

DINNER

....

....

....

SNACKS

....

....

....

WELL-WATERED

○ ○ ○ ○ ○ ○ ○ ○ ○ ○ ○ ○

GOOD FOR YOU!

....

....

....

....

KEEP TRYING

....

....

....

....

EVEN THOUGH YOU HAVE LEARNED THE SKILL OF
RUNNING ON EMPTY, NOW IS THE TIME TO LEARN THE
ART OF BREATHING DEEP ALL OVER AGAIN.

−MORGAN HARPER NICHOLS

POSITIVE THOUGHTS

ENERGIZING CHOICES

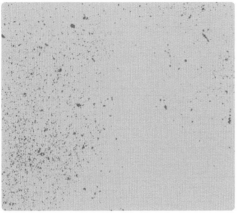

TIME IN NATURE

....

....

....

SOCIAL CONNECTIONS

....

....

ACTIVE DAY

BRAIN BOOSTS

....

....

....

SELF CHECK-INS

....

....

....

CLEAR MIND

JOY & GRATITUDE

....

....

....

RESTFUL SLEEP

....

....

....

INTENTIONAL EATING

BREAKFAST

....
....
....

LUNCH

....
....
....

DINNER

....
....
....

SNACKS

....
....
....

WELL-WATERED

◯ ◯ ◯ ◯ ◯ ◯ ◯ ◯ ◯ ◯ ◯ ◯

GOOD FOR YOU!

....
....
....
....

KEEP TRYING

....
....
....
....

ASK FOR HELP.
WHETHER YOU'RE TRYING TO LEARN A NEW SKILL,
JUGGLE ALL THE APPOINTMENTS ON YOUR
CALENDAR, OR SIMPLY STAY SANE, ASK FRIENDS,
FAMILY, AND PROFESSIONALS FOR WHAT YOU NEED.

POSITIVE THOUGHTS

ENERGIZING CHOICES

TIME IN NATURE

....

....

....

SOCIAL CONNECTIONS

....

....

....

ACTIVE DAY

BRAIN BOOSTS

....

....

....

SELF CHECK-INS

....

....

....

CLEAR MIND

JOY & GRATITUDE

....

....

....

RESTFUL SLEEP

....

....

....

INTENTIONAL EATING

BREAKFAST

....

....

....

LUNCH

....

....

....

DINNER

....

....

....

SNACKS

....

....

....

WELL-WATERED

○ ○ ○ ○ ○ ○ ○ ○ ○ ○ ○ ○

GOOD FOR YOU!

....

....

....

....

....

KEEP TRYING

....

....

....

....

....

WE ARE OUR OWN POTTERS;
FOR OUR HABITS MAKE US, AND WE
MAKE OUR HABITS.

–FREDERICK LANGBRIDGE

POSITIVE THOUGHTS

ACTIVE DAY

CLEAR MIND

ENERGIZING CHOICES

TIME IN NATURE

....

....

....

SOCIAL CONNECTIONS

....

....

....

BRAIN BOOSTS

....

....

....

SELF CHECK-INS

....

....

....

JOY & GRATITUDE

....

....

....

RESTFUL SLEEP

....

....

....

INTENTIONAL EATING

BREAKFAST

....
....
....

LUNCH

....
....
....

DINNER

....
....
....

SNACKS

....
....
....

WELL-WATERED

◯ ◯ ◯ ◯ ◯ ◯ ◯ ◯ ◯ ◯ ◯ ◯

GOOD FOR YOU!

....
....
....
....

KEEP TRYING

....
....
....
....

TRADE YOUR TIME.
COMMIT TO CUTTING SOME MINUTES FROM YOUR
ONLINE TIME TODAY. PROMISE YOURSELF A WAY
TO SPEND THOSE MINUTES THAT WILL FEED
YOUR WELLNESS.

POSITIVE THOUGHTS

ACTIVE DAY

CLEAR MIND

ENERGIZING CHOICES

TIME IN NATURE

....
....
....

SOCIAL CONNECTIONS

....
....
....

BRAIN BOOSTS

....
....
....

SELF CHECK-INS

....
....
....

JOY & GRATITUDE

....
....
....

RESTFUL SLEEP

....
....
....

INTENTIONAL EATING

BREAKFAST

....

....

....

LUNCH

....

....

....

DINNER

....

....

....

SNACKS

....

....

....

WELL-WATERED

○ ○ ○ ○ ○ ○ ○ ○ ○ ○ ○ ○

GOOD FOR YOU!

....

....

....

....

KEEP TRYING

....

....

....

....

TO BRING ANYTHING INTO YOUR LIFE,
IMAGINE THAT IT'S ALREADY THERE.

–RICHARD BACH

DATE .... M T W TH F SAT SUN

POSITIVE THOUGHTS

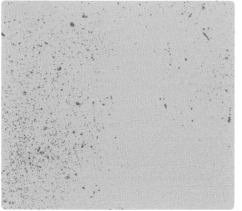

ACTIVE DAY

CLEAR MIND

ENERGIZING CHOICES

TIME IN NATURE

....

....

....

SOCIAL CONNECTIONS

....

....

....

BRAIN BOOSTS

....

....

....

SELF CHECK-INS

....

....

....

JOY & GRATITUDE

....

....

....

RESTFUL SLEEP

....

....

....

INTENTIONAL EATING

BREAKFAST

....
....
....

LUNCH

....
....
....

DINNER

....
....
....

SNACKS

....
....
....

WELL-WATERED

○ ○ ○ ○ ○ ○ ○ ○ ○ ○ ○ ○

GOOD FOR YOU!

....
....
....
....
....

KEEP TRYING

....
....
....
....
....

COME HOME TO COMFORT.
CHOOSE A TRANSITION INTO RELAXATION AFTER
AN ON-THE-GO DAY—MAYBE MAKE A CUP OF
TEA, TAKE A WALK, OR LIGHT A CANDLE.
YOU DESERVE IT!

POSITIVE THOUGHTS

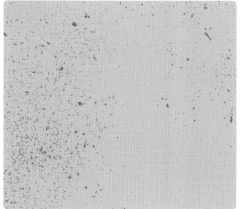

ACTIVE DAY

CLEAR MIND

ENERGIZING CHOICES

TIME IN NATURE

....

....

....

SOCIAL CONNECTIONS

....

....

....

BRAIN BOOSTS

....

....

....

SELF CHECK-INS

....

....

....

JOY & GRATITUDE

....

....

....

RESTFUL SLEEP

....

....

....

INTENTIONAL EATING

BREAKFAST

....
....
....

LUNCH

....
....
....

DINNER

....
....
....

SNACKS

....
....
....

WELL-WATERED

GOOD FOR YOU!

....
....
....
....
....

KEEP TRYING

....
....
....
....
....

IT IS HEALTH THAT IS REAL WEALTH AND NOT PIECES OF GOLD AND SILVER.

-MAHATMA GANDHI

POSITIVE THOUGHTS

ACTIVE DAY

CLEAR MIND

ENERGIZING CHOICES

TIME IN NATURE

SOCIAL CONNECTIONS

BRAIN BOOSTS

SELF CHECK-INS

JOY & GRATITUDE

RESTFUL SLEEP

INTENTIONAL EATING

BREAKFAST

....
....
....

LUNCH

....
....
....

DINNER

....
....
....

SNACKS

....
....
....

WELL-WATERED

○ ○ ○ ○ ○ ○ ○ ○ ○ ○ ○ ○

GOOD FOR YOU!

....
....
....
....

KEEP TRYING

....
....
....
....

FORGIVE YOURSELF.
EVERYONE HAS DAYS THAT DON'T ALIGN WITH
THEIR GOALS. LOOK AT WHAT MAY HAVE GOTTEN
YOU OFF TRACK, THEN MOVE ON AND TRY
AGAIN TOMORROW.

DATE .... M T W TH F SAT SUN

POSITIVE THOUGHTS

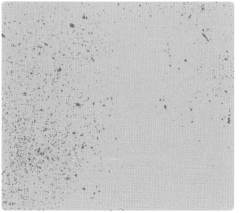

ACTIVE DAY

CLEAR MIND

ENERGIZING CHOICES

TIME IN NATURE

....

....

....

SOCIAL CONNECTIONS

....

....

....

BRAIN BOOSTS

....

....

....

SELF CHECK-INS

....

....

....

JOY & GRATITUDE

....

....

....

RESTFUL SLEEP

....

....

....

INTENTIONAL EATING

BREAKFAST

....

....

....

LUNCH

....

....

....

DINNER

....

....

....

SNACKS

....

....

....

WELL-WATERED

○ ○ ○ ○ ○ ○ ○ ○ ○ ○ ○ ○

GOOD FOR YOU!

....

....

....

....

KEEP TRYING

....

....

....

....

EVERY MORNING, LOOK IN THE MIRROR AND
AFFIRM POSITIVE WORDS INTO YOUR LIFE.

—LAILAH GIFTY AKITA

DATE .... M T W TH F SAT SUN

POSITIVE THOUGHTS

ACTIVE DAY

CLEAR MIND

ENERGIZING CHOICES

TIME IN NATURE

....
....
....

SOCIAL CONNECTIONS

....
....
....

BRAIN BOOSTS

....
....
....

SELF CHECK-INS

....
....
....

JOY & GRATITUDE

....
....
....

RESTFUL SLEEP

....
....
....

INTENTIONAL EATING

BREAKFAST
....
....
....

LUNCH
....
....
....

DINNER
....
....
....

SNACKS
....
....
....

WELL-WATERED

〇 〇 〇 〇 〇 〇 〇 〇 〇 〇 〇 〇

GOOD FOR YOU!
....
....
....
....

KEEP TRYING
....
....
....
....

PEP UP WITH PEPPERMINT.
ENERGY LAGGING? PEPPERMINT CAN BOOST MENTAL
ALERTNESS AND FITNESS ENDURANCE. TRY IT AS
A TEA OR AN ESSENTIAL OIL SCENT.

DATE .... M T W TH F SAT SUN

POSITIVE THOUGHTS

ACTIVE DAY

CLEAR MIND

ENERGIZING CHOICES

TIME IN NATURE

....

....

....

SOCIAL CONNECTIONS

....

....

....

BRAIN BOOSTS

....

....

....

SELF CHECK-INS

....

....

....

JOY & GRATITUDE

....

....

....

RESTFUL SLEEP

....

....

....

INTENTIONAL EATING

BREAKFAST

....
....
....

DINNER

....
....
....

LUNCH

....
....
....

SNACKS

....
....
....

WELL-WATERED

○ ○ ○ ○ ○ ○ ○ ○ ○ ○ ○ ○

GOOD FOR YOU!

....
....
....
....
....

KEEP TRYING

....
....
....
....
....

MY MISSION IN LIFE IS NOT MERELY TO SURVIVE,
BUT TO THRIVE; AND TO DO SO WITH
SOME PASSION, SOME COMPASSION,
SOME HUMOR, AND SOME STYLE.

−MAYA ANGELOU

POSITIVE THOUGHTS

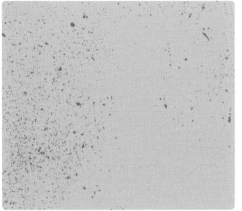

ACTIVE DAY

CLEAR MIND

ENERGIZING CHOICES

TIME IN NATURE

....

....

....

SOCIAL CONNECTIONS

....

....

....

BRAIN BOOSTS

....

....

....

SELF CHECK-INS

....

....

....

JOY & GRATITUDE

....

....

....

RESTFUL SLEEP

....

....

....

INTENTIONAL EATING

BREAKFAST

....

....

....

DINNER

....

....

....

LUNCH

....

....

....

SNACKS

....

....

....

WELL-WATERED

○ ○ ○ ○ ○ ○ ○ ○ ○ ○ ○ ○

GOOD FOR YOU!

....

....

....

....

KEEP TRYING

....

....

....

....

CATCH SOME RAYS.
IF YOU CAN, STEP OUTSIDE FOR LUNCH OR A
MIDDAY BREAK. YOU ONLY NEED A SHORT TIME
(AROUND 10 MINUTES) IN THE SUN TO GET THE
VITAMIN D BENEFITS WITHOUT THE SUNBURN.

DATE .... M T W TH F SAT SUN

POSITIVE THOUGHTS

ENERGIZING CHOICES

TIME IN NATURE

....

....

....

SOCIAL CONNECTIONS

....

....

....

ACTIVE DAY

BRAIN BOOSTS

....

....

....

SELF CHECK-INS

....

....

....

CLEAR MIND

JOY & GRATITUDE

....

....

....

RESTFUL SLEEP

....

....

....

INTENTIONAL EATING

BREAKFAST

....

....

....

LUNCH

....

....

....

DINNER

....

....

....

SNACKS

....

....

....

WELL-WATERED

○ ○ ○ ○ ○ ○ ○ ○ ○ ○ ○ ○

GOOD FOR YOU!

....

....

....

....

KEEP TRYING

....

....

....

....

THE SUN, THE EARTH, LOVE, FRIENDS,
OUR VERY BREATH ARE PARTS OF THE BANQUET.

–REBECCA HARDING DAVIS

DATE .... M T W TH F SAT SUN

POSITIVE THOUGHTS

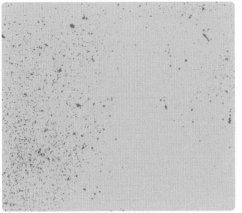

ACTIVE DAY

CLEAR MIND

ENERGIZING CHOICES

TIME IN NATURE

....

....

....

SOCIAL CONNECTIONS

....

....

....

BRAIN BOOSTS

....

....

....

SELF CHECK-INS

....

....

....

JOY & GRATITUDE

....

....

....

RESTFUL SLEEP

....

....

....

INTENTIONAL EATING

BREAKFAST

....

....

....

LUNCH

....

....

....

DINNER

....

....

....

SNACKS

....

....

....

WELL-WATERED

GOOD FOR YOU!

....

....

....

....

KEEP TRYING

....

....

....

....

GREET A GREAT MOOD.
THROUGHOUT YOUR DAY, SHARE FRIENDLY
GREETINGS WITH AS MANY PEOPLE AS YOU CAN.
SMILE, WAVE, SAY HELLO. SEE IF IT MAKES A
DIFFERENCE IN YOUR MOOD.

DATE .... M T W TH F SAT SUN

POSITIVE THOUGHTS

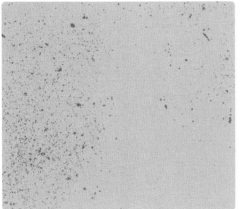

ACTIVE DAY

CLEAR MIND

ENERGIZING CHOICES

TIME IN NATURE

....

....

....

SOCIAL CONNECTIONS

....

....

....

BRAIN BOOSTS

....

....

....

SELF CHECK-INS

....

....

....

JOY & GRATITUDE

....

....

....

RESTFUL SLEEP

....

....

....

INTENTIONAL EATING

BREAKFAST

....

....

....

LUNCH

....

....

....

DINNER

....

....

....

SNACKS

....

....

....

WELL-WATERED

◯ ◯ ◯ ◯ ◯ ◯ ◯ ◯ ◯ ◯ ◯ ◯

GOOD FOR YOU!

....

....

....

....

KEEP TRYING

....

....

....

....

TODAY WAS GOOD. TODAY WAS FUN.
TOMORROW IS ANOTHER ONE.

–DR. SEUSS

DATE .... M T W TH F SAT SUN

POSITIVE THOUGHTS

ACTIVE DAY

CLEAR MIND

ENERGIZING CHOICES

TIME IN NATURE

....

....

....

SOCIAL CONNECTIONS

....

....

....

BRAIN BOOSTS

....

....

....

SELF CHECK-INS

....

....

....

JOY & GRATITUDE

....

....

....

RESTFUL SLEEP

....

....

....

INTENTIONAL EATING

BREAKFAST

....

....

....

DINNER

....

....

....

LUNCH

....

....

....

SNACKS

....

....

....

WELL-WATERED

○ ○ ○ ○ ○ ○ ○ ○ ○ ○ ○ ○

GOOD FOR YOU!

....

....

....

....

KEEP TRYING

....

....

....

....

PICK A PLAYLIST.
WHATEVER TOUGH TASK YOU'RE FACING—WHETHER
A HARD WORKOUT, A SERIOUS CONVERSATION,
OR A WORK DEADLINE—BUILD YOURSELF UP
WITH MUSIC.

POSITIVE THOUGHTS

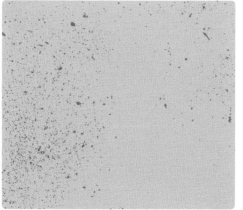

ACTIVE DAY

CLEAR MIND

ENERGIZING CHOICES

TIME IN NATURE

....

....

....

SOCIAL CONNECTIONS

....

....

....

BRAIN BOOSTS

....

....

....

SELF CHECK-INS

....

....

....

JOY & GRATITUDE

....

....

....

RESTFUL SLEEP

....

....

....

INTENTIONAL EATING

BREAKFAST

....

....

....

DINNER

....

....

....

LUNCH

....

....

....

SNACKS

....

....

....

WELL-WATERED

GOOD FOR YOU!

....

....

....

....

KEEP TRYING

....

....

....

....

AS LONG AS YOU LIVE,
KEEP LEARNING HOW TO LIVE.

-SENECA

DATE .... M T W TH F SAT SUN

POSITIVE THOUGHTS

ENERGIZING CHOICES

TIME IN NATURE

....

....

....

SOCIAL CONNECTIONS

....

....

ACTIVE DAY

BRAIN BOOSTS

....

....

SELF CHECK-INS

....

....

CLEAR MIND

JOY & GRATITUDE

....

....

RESTFUL SLEEP

....

....

....

INTENTIONAL EATING

BREAKFAST

....

....

....

LUNCH

....

....

....

DINNER

....

....

....

SNACKS

....

....

....

WELL-WATERED

○ ○ ○ ○ ○ ○ ○ ○ ○ ○ ○ ○

GOOD FOR YOU!

....

....

....

....

KEEP TRYING

....

....

....

....

BLOCK THE BLUE.
BLUE LIGHT FROM E-DEVICES CAN SUPPRESS
MELATONIN, WHICH CAN DISRUPT YOUR NATURAL
SLEEP CYCLE. IF YOU CAN'T TURN OFF
ELECTRONICS 30 TO 60 MINUTES BEFORE BED,
TRY BLUE LIGHT-BLOCKING GLASSES OR FILTERS.

POSITIVE THOUGHTS

ACTIVE DAY

CLEAR MIND

ENERGIZING CHOICES

TIME IN NATURE

SOCIAL CONNECTIONS

BRAIN BOOSTS

SELF CHECK-INS

JOY & GRATITUDE

RESTFUL SLEEP

INTENTIONAL EATING

BREAKFAST

....
....
....

DINNER

....
....
....

LUNCH

....
....
....

SNACKS

....
....
....

WELL-WATERED

○ ○ ○ ○ ○ ○ ○ ○ ○ ○ ○ ○

GOOD FOR YOU!

....
....
....
....

KEEP TRYING

....
....
....
....

YOUR BODY IS NOT YOUR ART,
IT'S YOUR PAINTBRUSH.

–GLENNON DOYLE

DATE .... M T W TH F SAT SUN

POSITIVE THOUGHTS

ACTIVE DAY

CLEAR MIND

ENERGIZING CHOICES

TIME IN NATURE

....
....
....

SOCIAL CONNECTIONS

....
....
....

BRAIN BOOSTS

....
....
....

SELF CHECK-INS

....
....
....

JOY & GRATITUDE

....
....
....

RESTFUL SLEEP

....
....
....

INTENTIONAL EATING

BREAKFAST

....

....

....

DINNER

....

....

....

LUNCH

....

....

....

SNACKS

....

....

....

WELL-WATERED

○ ○ ○ ○ ○ ○ ○ ○ ○ ○ ○ ○

GOOD FOR YOU!

....

....

....

....

KEEP TRYING

....

....

....

....

SOAK IN SOOTHING.
ADD 1 CUP OF EPSOM SALTS TO YOUR
BATHWATER TO RELIEVE STRESS, RELAX MUSCLES,
AND REDUCE INTERNAL INFLAMMATION.

DATE .... M T W TH F SAT SUN

POSITIVE THOUGHTS

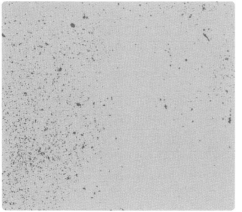

ACTIVE DAY

CLEAR MIND

ENERGIZING CHOICES

TIME IN NATURE

....

....

....

SOCIAL CONNECTIONS

....

....

....

BRAIN BOOSTS

....

....

....

SELF CHECK-INS

....

....

....

JOY & GRATITUDE

....

....

....

RESTFUL SLEEP

....

....

....

INTENTIONAL EATING

BREAKFAST

....
....
....

LUNCH

....
....
....

DINNER

....
....
....

SNACKS

....
....
....

WELL-WATERED

○ ○ ○ ○ ○ ○ ○ ○ ○ ○ ○ ○

GOOD FOR YOU!

....
....
....
....

KEEP TRYING

....
....
....
....

ALMOST EVERYTHING WILL WORK AGAIN
IF YOU UNPLUG IT FOR A FEW MINUTES,
INCLUDING YOU.

−ANNE LAMOTT

POSITIVE THOUGHTS

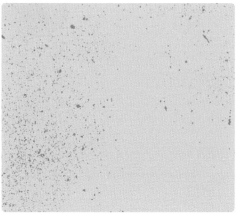

ACTIVE DAY

CLEAR MIND

ENERGIZING CHOICES

TIME IN NATURE

SOCIAL CONNECTIONS

BRAIN BOOSTS

SELF CHECK-INS

JOY & GRATITUDE

RESTFUL SLEEP

INTENTIONAL EATING

BREAKFAST

LUNCH

DINNER

SNACKS

WELL-WATERED

GOOD FOR YOU!

KEEP TRYING

PLAN AN ESCAPE.
GIVE YOURSELF A BREAK FROM YOUR EVERYDAY
RESPONSIBILITIES BY GETTING AWAY EVERY NOW AND
THEN. EVEN THE ANTICIPATION YOU FEEL IN THE
TRIP-PLANNING PROCESS CAN RELIEVE STRESS.

POSITIVE THOUGHTS

ACTIVE DAY

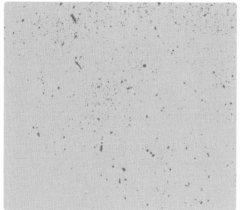

CLEAR MIND

ENERGIZING CHOICES

TIME IN NATURE

....

....

....

SOCIAL CONNECTIONS

....

....

....

BRAIN BOOSTS

....

....

....

SELF CHECK-INS

....

....

....

JOY & GRATITUDE

....

....

....

RESTFUL SLEEP

....

....

....

INTENTIONAL EATING

BREAKFAST

....

....

....

LUNCH

....

....

....

DINNER

....

....

....

SNACKS

....

....

....

WELL-WATERED

○ ○ ○ ○ ○ ○ ○ ○ ○ ○ ○ ○

GOOD FOR YOU!

....

....

....

....

KEEP TRYING

....

....

....

....

WE HAVE TO PROTECT OUR MIND
AND OUR BODY, RATHER THAN JUST GO OUT
THERE AND DO WHAT THE WORLD
WANTS US TO DO.

—SIMONE BILES

DATE .... M T W TH F SAT SUN

POSITIVE THOUGHTS

ACTIVE DAY

CLEAR MIND

ENERGIZING CHOICES

TIME IN NATURE

....
....
....

SOCIAL CONNECTIONS

....
....
....

BRAIN BOOSTS

....
....
....

SELF CHECK-INS

....
....
....

JOY & GRATITUDE

....
....
....

RESTFUL SLEEP

....
....
....

INTENTIONAL EATING

BREAKFAST

....

....

....

LUNCH

....

....

....

DINNER

....

....

....

SNACKS

....

....

....

WELL-WATERED

○ ○ ○ ○ ○ ○ ○ ○ ○ ○ ○ ○

GOOD FOR YOU!

....

....

....

....

KEEP TRYING

....

....

....

....

GO "PRO."
STRENGTHEN YOUR IMMUNE SYSTEM WITH
PROBIOTIC-RICH FOODS AND DRINKS. TRY KIMCHI,
KOMBUCHA, KEFIR, MISO, PICKLES, SAUERKRAUT,
TEMPEH, AND UNSWEETENED GREEK YOGURT.

POSITIVE THOUGHTS

ACTIVE DAY

CLEAR MIND

ENERGIZING CHOICES

TIME IN NATURE

....

....

....

SOCIAL CONNECTIONS

....

....

....

BRAIN BOOSTS

....

....

....

SELF CHECK-INS

....

....

....

JOY & GRATITUDE

....

....

....

RESTFUL SLEEP

....

....

....

INTENTIONAL EATING

BREAKFAST

....

....

....

LUNCH

....

....

....

DINNER

....

....

....

SNACKS

....

....

....

WELL-WATERED

GOOD FOR YOU!

....

....

....

....

KEEP TRYING

....

....

....

....

YOUR HAPPINESS LIES
IN YOUR HANDS.

–TARAJI P. HENSON

POSITIVE THOUGHTS

ACTIVE DAY

CLEAR MIND

ENERGIZING CHOICES

TIME IN NATURE

....

....

....

SOCIAL CONNECTIONS

....

....

....

BRAIN BOOSTS

....

....

....

SELF CHECK-INS

....

....

....

JOY & GRATITUDE

....

....

....

RESTFUL SLEEP

....

....

....

INTENTIONAL EATING

BREAKFAST

....
....
....

LUNCH

....
....
....

DINNER

....
....
....

SNACKS

....
....
....

WELL-WATERED

○ ○ ○ ○ ○ ○ ○ ○ ○ ○ ○ ○

GOOD FOR YOU!

....
....
....
....

KEEP TRYING

....
....
....
....

REVEL IN RECESS.
DO SOMETHING TODAY JUST FOR THE FUN OF IT.
NEED INSPIRATION? THINK ABOUT WHAT YOU ENJOYED
AS A CHILD—MAYBE COLORING, BIKE RIDING,
OR READING IN A BLANKET FORT.

DATE .... M T W TH F SAT SUN

POSITIVE THOUGHTS

ENERGIZING CHOICES

TIME IN NATURE

....

....

....

SOCIAL CONNECTIONS

....

....

....

ACTIVE DAY

BRAIN BOOSTS

....

....

....

SELF CHECK-INS

....

....

....

CLEAR MIND

JOY & GRATITUDE

....

....

....

RESTFUL SLEEP

....

....

....

INTENTIONAL EATING

BREAKFAST

....

....

....

LUNCH

....

....

....

DINNER

....

....

....

SNACKS

....

....

....

WELL-WATERED

○ ○ ○ ○ ○ ○ ○ ○ ○ ○ ○ ○

GOOD FOR YOU!

....

....

....

....

KEEP TRYING

....

....

....

....

YOU CAN'T STOP THE WAVES,
BUT YOU CAN LEARN TO SURF.

–JON KABAT-ZINN

POSITIVE THOUGHTS

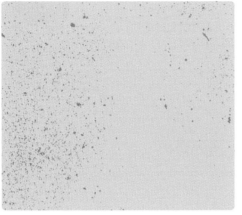

ACTIVE DAY

CLEAR MIND

ENERGIZING CHOICES

TIME IN NATURE

....

....

....

SOCIAL CONNECTIONS

....

....

....

BRAIN BOOSTS

....

....

....

SELF CHECK-INS

....

....

....

JOY & GRATITUDE

....

....

....

RESTFUL SLEEP

....

....

....

INTENTIONAL EATING

BREAKFAST

LUNCH

....

....

....

DINNER

SNACKS

....

....

....

WELL-WATERED

○ ○ ○ ○ ○ ○ ○ ○ ○ ○ ○ ○

GOOD FOR YOU!

KEEP TRYING

....

....

....

....

CARRY A CENTER.
CHOOSE A POCKET-SIZE OBJECT—MAYBE A STONE,
CRYSTAL, OR SHELL—THAT CAN GROUND YOU
THROUGH SIGHT OR TOUCH WHENEVER YOU FEEL
ANXIOUS OR UNSTEADY.

DATE .... M T W TH F SAT SUN

POSITIVE THOUGHTS

ACTIVE DAY

CLEAR MIND

ENERGIZING CHOICES

TIME IN NATURE

....
....
....

SOCIAL CONNECTIONS

....
....
....

BRAIN BOOSTS

....
....
....

SELF CHECK-INS

....
....
....

JOY & GRATITUDE

....
....
....

RESTFUL SLEEP

....
....
....

INTENTIONAL EATING

BREAKFAST

....
....
....

LUNCH

....
....
....

DINNER

....
....
....

SNACKS

....
....
....

WELL-WATERED

○ ○ ○ ○ ○ ○ ○ ○ ○ ○ ○ ○

GOOD FOR YOU!

....
....
....
....

KEEP TRYING

....
....
....
....

COURAGE OF THE HEART IS VERY RARE.
LET IT GUIDE YOU.

−SARAH J. MAAS

DATE .... M T W TH F SAT SUN

POSITIVE THOUGHTS

ACTIVE DAY

CLEAR MIND

ENERGIZING CHOICES

TIME IN NATURE

....

....

....

SOCIAL CONNECTIONS

....

....

....

BRAIN BOOSTS

....

....

....

SELF CHECK-INS

....

....

....

JOY & GRATITUDE

....

....

....

RESTFUL SLEEP

....

....

....

INTENTIONAL EATING

BREAKFAST

....
....
....

LUNCH

....
....
....

DINNER

....
....
....

SNACKS

....
....
....

WELL-WATERED

○ ○ ○ ○ ○ ○ ○ ○ ○ ○ ○ ○

GOOD FOR YOU!

....
....
....
....

KEEP TRYING

....
....
....
....

WRITE A THANK-YOU NOTE.
TRY GOING OLD-SCHOOL WITH PEN AND PRETTY
PAPER. GRATITUDE INCREASES HAPPINESS AND
CONTRIBUTES TO PHYSICAL HEALTH, TOO.

DATE .... M T W TH F SAT SUN

POSITIVE THOUGHTS

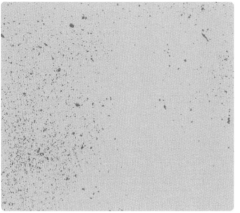

ACTIVE DAY

CLEAR MIND

ENERGIZING CHOICES

TIME IN NATURE

....

....

....

SOCIAL CONNECTIONS

....

....

....

BRAIN BOOSTS

....

....

....

SELF CHECK-INS

....

....

....

JOY & GRATITUDE

....

....

....

RESTFUL SLEEP

....

....

....

INTENTIONAL EATING

BREAKFAST

....
....
....

LUNCH

....
....
....

DINNER

....
....
....

SNACKS

....
....
....

WELL-WATERED

○ ○ ○ ○ ○ ○ ○ ○ ○ ○ ○ ○

GOOD FOR YOU!

....
....
....
....

KEEP TRYING

....
....
....
....

ASK WHAT MAKES YOU COME ALIVE,
AND GO DO IT.

—HOWARD THURMAN

POSITIVE THOUGHTS

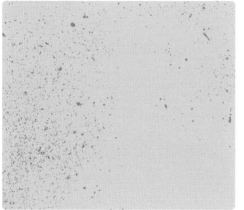

ACTIVE DAY

CLEAR MIND

ENERGIZING CHOICES

TIME IN NATURE

....

....

....

SOCIAL CONNECTIONS

....

....

....

BRAIN BOOSTS

....

....

....

SELF CHECK-INS

....

....

....

JOY & GRATITUDE

....

....

....

RESTFUL SLEEP

....

....

....

INTENTIONAL EATING

BREAKFAST

....

....

....

LUNCH

....

....

....

DINNER

....

....

....

SNACKS

....

....

....

WELL-WATERED

○ ○ ○ ○ ○ ○ ○ ○ ○ ○ ○ ○

GOOD FOR YOU!

....

....

....

....

KEEP TRYING

....

....

....

....

FIND SOME QUIET.
MAP OUT SOMEWHERE YOU CAN GO TODAY
(EVEN IF FOR JUST A FEW MINUTES) TO SILENCE
THE MADNESS OF SCHEDULES AND EXPECTATIONS.

DATE .... M T W TH F SAT SUN

POSITIVE THOUGHTS

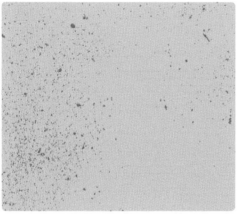

ACTIVE DAY

CLEAR MIND

ENERGIZING CHOICES

TIME IN NATURE

....

....

....

SOCIAL CONNECTIONS

....

....

....

BRAIN BOOSTS

....

....

....

SELF CHECK-INS

....

....

....

JOY & GRATITUDE

....

....

....

RESTFUL SLEEP

....

....

....

INTENTIONAL EATING

BREAKFAST

....

....

....

DINNER

....

....

....

LUNCH

....

....

....

SNACKS

....

....

....

WELL-WATERED

○ ○ ○ ○ ○ ○ ○ ○ ○ ○ ○ ○

GOOD FOR YOU!

....

....

....

....

KEEP TRYING

....

....

....

....

NOTHING IS WORTH MORE THAN LAUGHTER.
IT IS STRENGTH TO LAUGH AND TO ABANDON
ONESELF, TO BE LIGHT.

—FRIDA KAHLO

DATE .... M T W TH F SAT SUN

POSITIVE THOUGHTS

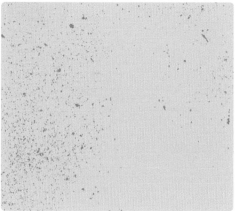

ACTIVE DAY

CLEAR MIND

ENERGIZING CHOICES

TIME IN NATURE

....

....

....

SOCIAL CONNECTIONS

....

....

....

BRAIN BOOSTS

....

....

....

SELF CHECK-INS

....

....

....

JOY & GRATITUDE

....

....

....

RESTFUL SLEEP

....

....

....

INTENTIONAL EATING

BREAKFAST

....

....

....

LUNCH

....

....

....

DINNER

....

....

....

SNACKS

....

....

....

WELL-WATERED

○ ○ ○ ○ ○ ○ ○ ○ ○ ○ ○ ○

GOOD FOR YOU!

....

....

....

....

KEEP TRYING

....

....

....

....

POST A NOTE.

WHAT DO YOU WANT TO TELL YOURSELF TODAY—MAYBE
YOU NEED MORE FRESH AIR? STICK A REMINDER
SOMEWHERE YOU'LL SEE IT AT LEAST A FEW
TIMES THROUGHOUT THE DAY.

POSITIVE THOUGHTS

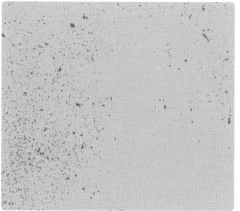

ACTIVE DAY

CLEAR MIND

ENERGIZING CHOICES

TIME IN NATURE

....

....

....

SOCIAL CONNECTIONS

....

....

....

BRAIN BOOSTS

....

....

....

SELF CHECK-INS

....

....

....

JOY & GRATITUDE

....

....

....

RESTFUL SLEEP

....

....

....

INTENTIONAL EATING

BREAKFAST

....

....

....

LUNCH

....

....

....

DINNER

....

....

....

SNACKS

....

....

....

WELL-WATERED

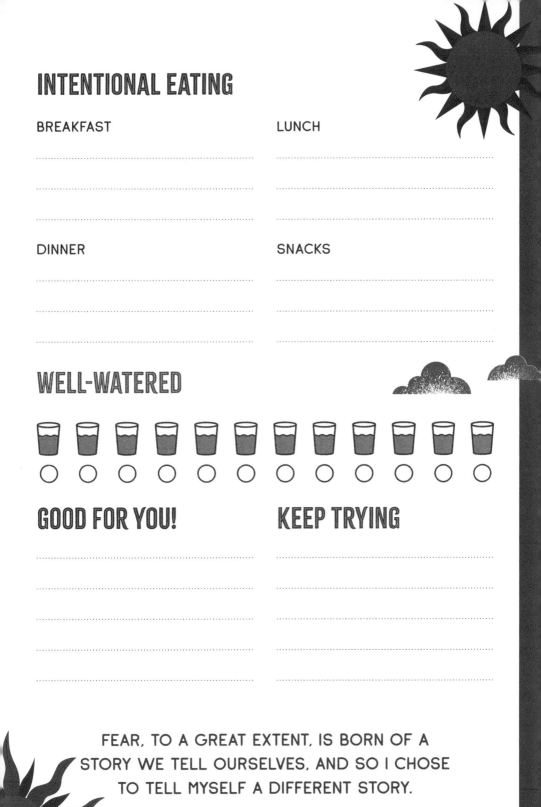

GOOD FOR YOU!

....

....

....

....

KEEP TRYING

....

....

....

....

FEAR, TO A GREAT EXTENT, IS BORN OF A
STORY WE TELL OURSELVES, AND SO I CHOSE
TO TELL MYSELF A DIFFERENT STORY.

–CHERYL STRAYED

POSITIVE THOUGHTS

ACTIVE DAY

CLEAR MIND

ENERGIZING CHOICES

TIME IN NATURE

....

....

....

SOCIAL CONNECTIONS

....

....

....

BRAIN BOOSTS

....

....

....

SELF CHECK-INS

....

....

....

JOY & GRATITUDE

....

....

....

RESTFUL SLEEP

....

....

....

INTENTIONAL EATING

BREAKFAST

....
....
....

LUNCH

....
....
....

DINNER

....
....
....

SNACKS

....
....
....

WELL-WATERED

○ ○ ○ ○ ○ ○ ○ ○ ○ ○ ○ ○

GOOD FOR YOU!

....
....
....
....

KEEP TRYING

....
....
....
....

STAY OPEN.
AS YOU GO TOWARD A GOAL, YOUR GUT MAY
TELL YOU THAT YOU'RE HEADING IN THE
WRONG DIRECTION. WHEN NEW PATHS REVEAL
THEMSELVES TO YOU, GIVE YOURSELF
PERMISSION TO TAKE THEM.

POSITIVE THOUGHTS

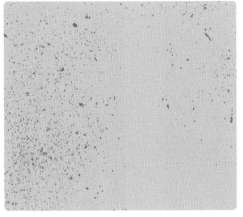

ACTIVE DAY

CLEAR MIND

ENERGIZING CHOICES

TIME IN NATURE

....

....

....

SOCIAL CONNECTIONS

....

....

....

BRAIN BOOSTS

....

....

....

SELF CHECK-INS

....

....

....

JOY & GRATITUDE

....

....

....

RESTFUL SLEEP

....

....

....

INTENTIONAL EATING

BREAKFAST

....

....

....

LUNCH

....

....

....

DINNER

....

....

....

SNACKS

....

....

....

WELL-WATERED

○ ○ ○ ○ ○ ○ ○ ○ ○ ○ ○ ○

GOOD FOR YOU!

....

....

....

....

KEEP TRYING

....

....

....

....

THIS REVOLUTIONARY ACT OF TREATING
OURSELVES TENDERLY CAN BEGIN TO UNDO THE
AVERSIVE MESSAGES OF A LIFETIME.

–TARA BRACH

DATE .... M T W TH F SAT SUN

POSITIVE THOUGHTS

ACTIVE DAY

CLEAR MIND

ENERGIZING CHOICES

TIME IN NATURE

....

....

....

SOCIAL CONNECTIONS

....

....

....

BRAIN BOOSTS

....

....

....

SELF CHECK-INS

....

....

....

JOY & GRATITUDE

....

....

....

RESTFUL SLEEP

....

....

....

INTENTIONAL EATING

BREAKFAST

....

....

....

LUNCH

....

....

....

DINNER

....

....

....

SNACKS

....

....

....

WELL-WATERED

○ ○ ○ ○ ○ ○ ○ ○ ○ ○ ○ ○

GOOD FOR YOU!

....

....

....

....

KEEP TRYING

....

....

....

....

GIVE YOURSELF "GOOD ENOUGH."
EXPECTING PERFECTION CAN STOP YOU IN YOUR
TRACKS WITH FEAR. LET GO OF THE UNREALISTIC
SO YOU CAN ENJOY THE ACHIEVABLE.

DATE .... M T W TH F SAT SUN

POSITIVE THOUGHTS

ACTIVE DAY

CLEAR MIND

ENERGIZING CHOICES

TIME IN NATURE

....

....

....

SOCIAL CONNECTIONS

....

....

....

BRAIN BOOSTS

....

....

....

SELF CHECK-INS

....

....

....

JOY & GRATITUDE

....

....

....

RESTFUL SLEEP

....

....

....

INTENTIONAL EATING

BREAKFAST

....

....

....

LUNCH

....

....

....

DINNER

....

....

....

SNACKS

....

....

....

WELL-WATERED

GOOD FOR YOU!

....

....

....

....

....

KEEP TRYING

....

....

....

....

....

DO ANYTHING,
BUT LET IT PRODUCE JOY.

–WALT WHITMAN

DATE ....   M   T   W   TH   F   SAT   SUN

POSITIVE THOUGHTS

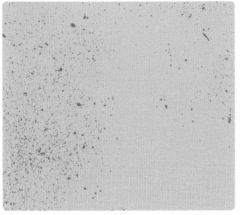

ACTIVE DAY

CLEAR MIND

ENERGIZING CHOICES

TIME IN NATURE

....

....

....

SOCIAL CONNECTIONS

....

....

....

BRAIN BOOSTS

....

....

....

SELF CHECK-INS

....

....

....

JOY & GRATITUDE

....

....

....

RESTFUL SLEEP

....

....

....

INTENTIONAL EATING

BREAKFAST

....

....

....

DINNER

....

....

....

LUNCH

....

....

....

SNACKS

....

....

....

WELL-WATERED

○ ○ ○ ○ ○ ○ ○ ○ ○ ○ ○ ○

GOOD FOR YOU!

....

....

....

....

KEEP TRYING

....

....

....

....

CLEAR THE CLUTTER.
FIND ONE THING YOU CAN CLEAR FROM YOUR
SCHEDULE OR PHYSICAL ENVIRONMENT TO MAKE ROOM
FOR SOMETHING NEW TO FUEL YOUR GOALS.

POSITIVE THOUGHTS

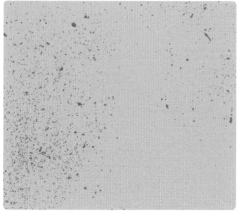

ACTIVE DAY

CLEAR MIND

ENERGIZING CHOICES

TIME IN NATURE

....

....

....

SOCIAL CONNECTIONS

....

....

....

BRAIN BOOSTS

....

....

....

SELF CHECK-INS

....

....

....

JOY & GRATITUDE

....

....

....

RESTFUL SLEEP

....

....

....

INTENTIONAL EATING

BREAKFAST

....

....

....

LUNCH

....

....

....

DINNER

....

....

....

SNACKS

....

....

....

WELL-WATERED

○ ○ ○ ○ ○ ○ ○ ○ ○ ○ ○ ○

GOOD FOR YOU!

....

....

....

....

KEEP TRYING

....

....

....

....

IF YOU KNOW THE ART OF DEEP BREATHING,
YOU HAVE THE STRENGTH, WISDOM,
AND COURAGE OF TEN TIGERS.

—CHINESE ADAGE

POSITIVE THOUGHTS

ENERGIZING CHOICES

TIME IN NATURE

....

....

....

SOCIAL CONNECTIONS

....

....

....

ACTIVE DAY

BRAIN BOOSTS

....

....

....

SELF CHECK-INS

....

....

....

CLEAR MIND

JOY & GRATITUDE

....

....

....

RESTFUL SLEEP

....

....

....

INTENTIONAL EATING

BREAKFAST

....

....

....

LUNCH

....

....

....

DINNER

....

....

....

SNACKS

....

....

....

WELL-WATERED

○ ○ ○ ○ ○ ○ ○ ○ ○ ○ ○ ○

GOOD FOR YOU!

....

....

....

....

KEEP TRYING

....

....

....

....

KNOW YOUR WORTH.
IN YOUR MIND OR ON PAPER, MAKE NOTE OF
TEN THINGS YOU LOVE ABOUT YOURSELF RIGHT
NOW—NO CONDITIONS OR CONTINGENCIES.

DATE .... M T W TH F SAT SUN

POSITIVE THOUGHTS

ACTIVE DAY

CLEAR MIND

ENERGIZING CHOICES

TIME IN NATURE

....

....

....

SOCIAL CONNECTIONS

....

....

....

BRAIN BOOSTS

....

....

....

SELF CHECK-INS

....

....

....

JOY & GRATITUDE

....

....

....

RESTFUL SLEEP

....

....

....

INTENTIONAL EATING

BREAKFAST

....

....

....

LUNCH

....

....

....

DINNER

....

....

....

SNACKS

....

....

....

WELL-WATERED

○ ○ ○ ○ ○ ○ ○ ○ ○ ○ ○ ○

GOOD FOR YOU!

....

....

....

....

KEEP TRYING

....

....

....

....

SELF-CARE IS HOW YOU TAKE
YOUR POWER BACK.

−LALAH DELIA

DATE .... M T W TH F SAT SUN

POSITIVE THOUGHTS

ACTIVE DAY

CLEAR MIND

ENERGIZING CHOICES

TIME IN NATURE

....

....

....

SOCIAL CONNECTIONS

....

....

....

BRAIN BOOSTS

....

....

....

SELF CHECK-INS

....

....

....

JOY & GRATITUDE

....

....

....

RESTFUL SLEEP

....

....

....

INTENTIONAL EATING

BREAKFAST

....
....
....

LUNCH

....
....
....

DINNER

....
....
....

SNACKS

....
....
....

WELL-WATERED

GOOD FOR YOU!

....
....
....
....

KEEP TRYING

....
....
....
....

LISTEN TO YOUR BODY.
WHAT DOES IT NEED TODAY? TREAT IT LIKE A GOOD
FRIEND AND RESPOND WITH LOVE AND ATTENTION
IN ANY FORM IT NEEDS.

DATE .... M T W TH F SAT SUN

POSITIVE THOUGHTS

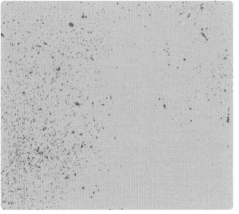

ACTIVE DAY

CLEAR MIND

ENERGIZING CHOICES

TIME IN NATURE

....

....

....

SOCIAL CONNECTIONS

....

....

....

BRAIN BOOSTS

....

....

....

SELF CHECK-INS

....

....

....

JOY & GRATITUDE

....

....

....

RESTFUL SLEEP

....

....

....

INTENTIONAL EATING

BREAKFAST

....
....
....

LUNCH

....
....
....

DINNER

....
....
....

SNACKS

....
....
....

WELL-WATERED

○ ○ ○ ○ ○ ○ ○ ○ ○ ○ ○ ○

GOOD FOR YOU!

....
....
....
....

KEEP TRYING

....
....
....
....

YOU ARE NOT WAITING FOR YOUR LIFE TO
START. IT'S GOING ON RIGHT NOW.

-JENNY SLATE

DATE .... M T W TH F SAT SUN

POSITIVE THOUGHTS

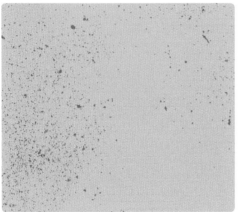

ENERGIZING CHOICES

TIME IN NATURE

....

....

....

SOCIAL CONNECTIONS

....

....

....

ACTIVE DAY

BRAIN BOOSTS

....

....

....

SELF CHECK-INS

....

....

....

CLEAR MIND

JOY & GRATITUDE

....

....

....

RESTFUL SLEEP

....

....

....

INTENTIONAL EATING

BREAKFAST

....

....

....

LUNCH

....

....

....

DINNER

....

....

....

SNACKS

....

....

....

WELL-WATERED

🥛 🥛 🥛 🥛 🥛 🥛 🥛 🥛 🥛 🥛 🥛 🥛

○ ○ ○ ○ ○ ○ ○ ○ ○ ○ ○ ○

GOOD FOR YOU!

....

....

....

....

KEEP TRYING

....

....

....

....

AUDIT YOUR APPS.
WHICH APPS HELP YOU REACH YOUR GOALS, AND
WHICH JUST SEEM TO ZAP YOUR TIME AND ENERGY?
STICK WITH ONLY WHAT SUPPORTS YOU; DELETE
THE REST.

DATE .... M T W TH F SAT SUN

POSITIVE THOUGHTS

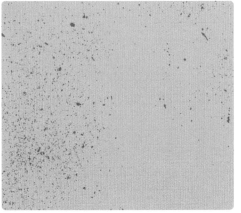

ACTIVE DAY

CLEAR MIND

ENERGIZING CHOICES

TIME IN NATURE

....

....

....

SOCIAL CONNECTIONS

....

....

....

BRAIN BOOSTS

....

....

....

SELF CHECK-INS

....

....

....

JOY & GRATITUDE

....

....

....

RESTFUL SLEEP

....

....

....

INTENTIONAL EATING

BREAKFAST

....
....
....

LUNCH

....
....
....

DINNER

....
....
....

SNACKS

....
....
....

WELL-WATERED

GOOD FOR YOU!

....
....
....
....
....

KEEP TRYING

....
....
....
....
....

HAPPINESS IS NOT A GOAL . . .
IT'S A BY-PRODUCT OF A LIFE WELL LIVED.

−ELEANOR ROOSEVELT

DATE .... M T W TH F SAT SUN

POSITIVE THOUGHTS

ACTIVE DAY

CLEAR MIND

ENERGIZING CHOICES

TIME IN NATURE

....

....

....

SOCIAL CONNECTIONS

....

....

....

BRAIN BOOSTS

....

....

....

SELF CHECK-INS

....

....

....

JOY & GRATITUDE

....

....

....

RESTFUL SLEEP

....

....

....

INTENTIONAL EATING

BREAKFAST

....

....

....

LUNCH

....

....

....

DINNER

....

....

....

SNACKS

....

....

....

WELL-WATERED

GOOD FOR YOU!

....

....

....

....

KEEP TRYING

....

....

....

....

BREATHE IN CALM.
TRY THE 4-7-8 TECHNIQUE: INHALE FOR 4 SECONDS,
HOLD YOUR BREATH FOR 7 SECONDS, AND THEN
EXHALE FOR 8 SECONDS. YOU'LL SEND A
RELAXATION SIGNAL TO YOUR BRAIN.

POSITIVE THOUGHTS

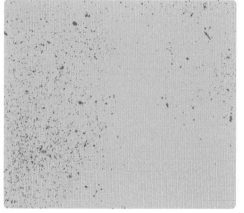

ACTIVE DAY

CLEAR MIND

ENERGIZING CHOICES

TIME IN NATURE

....
....
....

SOCIAL CONNECTIONS

....
....
....

BRAIN BOOSTS

....
....
....

SELF CHECK-INS

....
....
....

JOY & GRATITUDE

....
....
....

RESTFUL SLEEP

....
....
....

INTENTIONAL EATING

BREAKFAST

....
....
....

LUNCH

....
....
....

DINNER

....
....
....

SNACKS

....
....
....

WELL-WATERED

○ ○ ○ ○ ○ ○ ○ ○ ○ ○ ○ ○

GOOD FOR YOU!

....
....
....
....

KEEP TRYING

....
....
....
....

THE MOON IS NEVER MISSING ANY
OF ITSELF. WE JUST CAN'T SEE IT.
PEOPLE ARE LIKE THAT, TOO.

—JENNIFER PASTILOFF

DATE .... M T W TH F SAT SUN

POSITIVE THOUGHTS

ENERGIZING CHOICES

TIME IN NATURE

....

....

....

SOCIAL CONNECTIONS

....

....

....

ACTIVE DAY

BRAIN BOOSTS

....

....

....

SELF CHECK-INS

....

....

....

CLEAR MIND

JOY & GRATITUDE

....

....

....

RESTFUL SLEEP

....

....

....

INTENTIONAL EATING

BREAKFAST

....
....
....

LUNCH

....
....
....

DINNER

....
....
....

SNACKS

....
....
....

WELL-WATERED

○ ○ ○ ○ ○ ○ ○ ○ ○ ○ ○ ○

GOOD FOR YOU!

....
....
....
....

KEEP TRYING

....
....
....
....

JUMP OUT OF BED.
EACH MORNING, BEFORE YOUR FEET HIT THE FLOOR,
PICTURE IN YOUR MIND WHO OR WHAT YOU LOVE
MOST IN THIS WORLD.

DATE .... M T W TH F SAT SUN

POSITIVE THOUGHTS

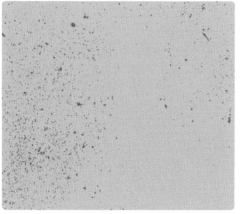

ACTIVE DAY

CLEAR MIND

ENERGIZING CHOICES

TIME IN NATURE

....

....

....

SOCIAL CONNECTIONS

....

....

....

BRAIN BOOSTS

....

....

....

SELF CHECK-INS

....

....

....

JOY & GRATITUDE

....

....

....

RESTFUL SLEEP

....

....

INTENTIONAL EATING

BREAKFAST

....
....
....

LUNCH

....
....
....

DINNER

....
....
....

SNACKS

....
....
....

WELL-WATERED

○ ○ ○ ○ ○ ○ ○ ○ ○ ○ ○ ○

GOOD FOR YOU!

....
....
....
....

KEEP TRYING

....
....
....
....

CARVE OUT AND CLAIM THE TIME
TO CARE FOR YOURSELF AND KINDLE
YOUR OWN FIRE.

—AMY IPPOLITI

POSITIVE THOUGHTS

ENERGIZING CHOICES

TIME IN NATURE

....

....

....

SOCIAL CONNECTIONS

....

....

....

ACTIVE DAY

BRAIN BOOSTS

....

....

....

SELF CHECK-INS

....

....

....

CLEAR MIND

JOY & GRATITUDE

....

....

....

RESTFUL SLEEP

....

....

....

INTENTIONAL EATING

BREAKFAST

....

....

....

LUNCH

....

....

....

DINNER

....

....

....

SNACKS

....

....

....

WELL-WATERED

○ ○ ○ ○ ○ ○ ○ ○ ○ ○ ○ ○

GOOD FOR YOU!

....

....

....

....

KEEP TRYING

....

....

....

....

HOLD SPACE FOR CELEBRATION.
NO MATTER HOW SMALL THE STEP FORWARD,
RECOGNIZE YOUR HEART, MIND, AND BODY FOR
MAKING THE MOVE.

GOOD FOR YOU FOR

★ Simply showing up every day as your amazing self

★ Making adjustments when life doesn't go as planned

★ Seeking your best path to healthy and happy living

XOXO, _____

(your signature and pledge to continue self-care)